For God, who said, "Light shall shine out of darkness," is the One who has shone in our hearts to give the Light of the knowledge of the glory of God in the face of Christ.

- 2 Corinthians 4:6

Examine Your Heart

Discipleship Study for Groups or Individuals

Envy
BLAME
ANGER
PRIDE
Doubt
FEAR
Lies
SiN
GREED
HATE
Control

Donna
LOWE
& Kimberly
SOESBEE

Touch Publishing

Published by Touch Publishing
P.O. Box 180303
Arlington, Texas 76096
www.TouchPublishingServices.com

Kimberly Soesbee photo by Lipsett Photography Group
www.KimberlySoesbee.com

Donna Lowe photo by Matt Ferguson
www.DonnaLowe.com

Cover designed by Touch Publishing

Look for *Radical Love... Forever Changed* through your local bookstore, online retailer, or through the authors
Radical Love ISBN: 978-0-9937951-2-1

Printed in the United States of America on acid-free paper

Table of Contents

Introduction

Are you craving more love? More passion? Intimacy? Does this sound like "relationship therapy 101?" It is, but not in the way you might be thinking.

We live in a culture that is at the same time obsessed with love and yet starved for the kind of love that changes lives for the better: God's love.

Several years ago, we wrote a book called *Radical Love... Forever Changed*. The message of *Radical Love* is threefold:

1. Without the Holy Spirit, it is impossible to love others with Jesus' love.
2. Once you have the Holy Spirit, there are things that can be barriers to loving ourselves and loving others radically.
3. We need to identify and bring those things to God for destruction.

Too many Christians go through their days in a spiritually dry state. Much like the bones found in the valley in Ezekiel 37, Christians in our church pews are dry, dry, dry. Intervention is required! The *Radical Love* book is a wonderful companion to this study. It isn't required to learn the truths presented in this book, however, we would recommend you get yourself (and maybe a friend) a copy.

To embark on this study, you need a Bible, a journal or notebook, something to write with, and ideally, a friend. You can do this study alone, however a small group or study partner provides accountability, fellowship, prayer covering, and the opportunity for discipleship.

The Need for Disciples

Accountability means you have someone who is dedicated to the same goal you are: in this case, getting to know Jesus better and learning to love more like He loves. Accountibility drives you to complete your study time when you are tempted to let other things slide in the schedule ahead of it.

Fellowship can be a balm when things around you pull you in different directions. It is friendship-building among people with shared interests and like mindsets.

Prayer is a powerful spiritual weapon against Satan. Speaking your needs out and joining together to lay them at the feet of Christ is a model seen throughout the New Testament.

Discipleship, however, is the hard work of the soul, where the sneakers meet the pavement and one believer comes alongside another believer for the purpose of growing his or her faith. It is sorely lacking in our congregations. Fellowship is not discipleship. Prayer meetings are not discipleship. Showing up is not discipleship. Friend, discipleship—learning and putting something into practice—is where things get interesting!

Together, with Christ's help, the messes of life can be made into something wonderful. The disagreements that threaten your countenance can be taken to God and put in right perspective. Places where you lack fruit of the Spirit can be identified and you can take steps to find Jesus and ask Him to help.

We'll say it again: Discipleship is hard work of the soul. That's why many Christians don't determinedly go after true discipleship relationships with one another. Churches whose members engage in this way with one another are evangelistic, growing, and impact their community without conforming to the community. They are becoming more and more like Christ. Why? Because Christ built disciples. The followers of Jesus are called "His **Disciples**." Christ's last spoken words recorded in Scripture were to "Go! And make **disciples**..."

Jesus cared deeply about discipleship. With that said, we encourage you to find at least one other brother or sister in Christ to work together through this 8 session study. If that simply is not possible, please connect with us (our contact info is at the back of the book) and know that we will be praying for you.

Lesson Structure:

There are 8 lessons in this book. Ideally, you'll complete one lesson in the course of a week's time, then meet together with your discipleship partner or small group and review your completed lessons. If your small group has a designated leader, the leader will find helpful advice for running a successful group beginning on page 85 of this study.

After each Lesson Introduction is a **Spicy Meatball**. The Spicy Meatball is a bold statement to which you may find you have a fleshly reaction. Spicy Meatballs can be difficult to digest. As such, the Spicy Meatball is the overriding truth we want you to grasp throughout the lesson.

Pay attention to how the Spicy Meatball makes you feel. What is your initial reaction to it? You'll want to discuss your initial thoughts in your group time, and identify how those thoughts change after you complete the rest of the lesson. When you embrace the biblical truth of the Spicy Meatball, you will experience growth.

Scripture Study time is where the Holy Spirit will speak to you through the word of God. We've left plenty of space for you to write in this book, so grab a pen and get to it. The Bible translation we reference most is the New American Standard Bible. If you use a different version, look the passage up in your Bible. Compare and contrast the words. Give God ample time and space to speak to you. We've intentionally sought not to overwhelm you with passages, but to look deeply into what is there, and find a truth you can apply immediately.

Life Application questions take the Scripture truths and guide you to make them personal. Grab a cup of coffee, take a deep breath, and open your heart. Examine it for places where time, life experience, failed relationships, or other disappointments have left wounds that need to heal. We don't want you to identify these wounds or areas of hurt to make you or anyone else feel badly. We want you to identify them because they may be places where there is a barrier between your version of love and the love that Jesus came to show. Our goal is that at the end of this study, you will be closer to Jesus and that you will find it increasingly easier to show God's love to those around you and to a lost and hurting world.

The **Journal** question is one we pray you'll spend time reflecting upon. Journaling is a personal exercise with no "right or wrongs." There are great benefits as you look back and see God's faithfulness, your own heart-healing and spiritual growth.

We may not know your name, but we are praying for you. God loves you.

Session 1
Expectations

LESSON INTRODUCTION

We have before us a two-fold, radical challenge:

1. We are to be unconditionally committed to Christ.
2. We are to be unconditionally committed to each other.

Beware: As simple as that sounds, it's deeply profound... and difficult, too! What prevents us from living out these two commitments? We're going to work through some of the barriers. Today, we begin with one word: expectations!

You see, no one is immune to disillusionment. We've all been let down by others, by ourselves, and even by God.

Have you ever scripted a dream and then played it out like a movie in your head? Envision it for a moment: You are in the leading role. Your written plot is complicated, twisting, and full of surprises and complexities. In your true(ish)-to-life dramatic piece, every character is crafted with tremendous attention to detail. Every word is chosen carefully; every action predetermined. Every scene is designed to evoke deep emotions.

Then... when it comes time for the movie to "go live," you extend invitations for auditions. Some people are hired based on first impressions, but you become frustrated when they don't play their parts right.

Why won't they stick to the written dialogue? you wonder.

The dialogue had unfolded flawlessly in your head. *Why is it that no one else knows the script except for you?*

You know that the right people are out there. So you fire those who don't measure up. There has to be those who are qualified and willing to play the part you need them to play, right? It will be worth the wait. You keep auditioning... and auditioning... You never stop to edit your script. The story was written down to the last page. You've seen the ending in your mind. You're clinging to its fulfillment! Now that you've seen it, you go after it for the rest of your life.

How's it *really* going to end? Here's a spoiler alert: It's extremely disappointing.

The reality is that we are flawed people who are in relationships with other flawed people. We all fail. Continuously. We forget our disappointments, so we renew our expectations, and then are surprised when we are disappointed all over again.

Disappointment is an overwhelming sadness caused by unfulfilled hopes or expectations. King Solomon said that *"hope deferred makes the heart sick."* (Proverbs 13:12) There are too many heart-sick people within the body of Christ. They are disappointed. Disillusioned. They carry unfulfilled hopes and dreams. With sad hearts, they walk away. From each other. And from Christ!

The church is called to be effective; to carry out the mission of Christ's radical love! Make no mistake loved one, Jesus wants to heal your heart so that you can love others. That is what this study is all about.

THE SPICY MEATBALL...
If you cling to your expectations of others, you
will choose to forfeit the miracle that awaits
you.

1. What questions come to mind when you read the above
statement? How does it make you feel?

SCRIPTURE STUDY

2 Kings 5:1-5:
Now Naaman, captain of the army of the king of Aram, was a
great man with his master, and highly respected, because by
him the Lord had given victory to Aram. The man was also a
valiant warrior, but he was a leper. 2 Now the Arameans had
gone out in bands and had taken captive a little girl from the
land of Israel; and she waited on Naaman's wife. 3 She said
to her mistress, "I wish that my master were with the
prophet who is in Samaria! Then he would cure him of his
leprosy." 4 Naaman went in and told his master, saying,
"Thus and thus spoke the girl who is from the land of Israel."
5 Then the king of Aram said, "Go now, and I will send a
letter to the king of Israel." He departed and took with him
ten talents of silver and six thousand shekels of gold and ten
changes of clothes.

2. What was Naaman's position?

3. How was Naaman regarded by others and why?

4. Circle what the king of Aram gave Naaman to take with him. What else did Naaman take with him?

5. Naaman had power, influence, and a lot of money. What do you think Naaman's self-perception might be?

2 Kings 5:6-7:
6 *He brought the letter to the king of Israel, saying, "And now as this letter comes to you, behold, I have sent Naaman my servant to you, that you may cure him of his leprosy."*7 *When the king of Israel read the letter, he tore his clothes and said, "Am I God, to kill and to make alive, that this man is sending word to me to cure a man of his leprosy? But consider now, and see how he is seeking a quarrel against me."*

As we'll see, there are many wrong expectations in this story. Feelings of self-importance play a large role in a person's expectations. No doubt the king of Aram imagined his will for Naaman would be carried out, simply because of who he was. In fact, it almost seems as though he is giving the king of Israel permission to heal Naaman.

6. How did the king of Israel react to the letter?

Wrongly placed expectations can put tremendous pressure on others. Often the requests we make are impossible, and we could not even fulfill them ourselves! Expectations and demands produce anxiety and hopelessness.

7. What accusation did the king of Israel make about the king of Aram? Was his speculation true?

The relationship between Aram and Israel was dysfunctional at best, but the two kings had an amicable relationship at the time this story played out. Even so, when people are asked to do too much or to do the impossible, they get suspicious.

Let's continue:

2 Kings 5:8-10:
8 *It happened when Elisha the man of God heard that the king of Israel had torn his clothes, that he sent word to the king, saying, "Why have you torn your clothes? Now let him come to me, and he shall know that there is a prophet in Israel."9 So Naaman came with his horses and his chariots and stood at the doorway of the house of Elisha. 10 Elisha sent a messenger to him, saying, "Go and wash in the Jordan seven times, and your flesh will be restored to you and you will be clean."*

8. Who brought the instructions regarding healing to Naaman? Circle the instructions given by Elisha to Naaman regarding how he would be healed.

2 Kings 5:11-12:
11 *But Naaman was furious and went away and said,
"Behold, I thought, 'He will surely come out to me and stand
and call on the name of the Lord his God, and wave his hand
over the place and cure the leper.' 12 Are not Abanah and
Pharpar, the rivers of Damascus, better than all the waters
of Israel? Could I not wash in them and be clean?" So he
turned and went away in a rage.*

9. What was Naaman's assumption?

10. Does Naaman's expectation as to how he would be
healed seem any more reasonable to you than Elisha's
instructions?

You need to see this: No one questioned whether or not
Naaman would be healed. Right from the beginning it
seemed healing was inevitable. The king of Israel
questioned his own ability to heal, but he never questioned
the plausibility of it. Even Naaman knew it would happen.

11. How did Naaman react when the "how" didn't match
his expectation? (see verse 12 above)

The image in Naaman's mind of how things should play out
was so powerful that when it didn't go his way, he was
willing to risk the miracle—his own health. At the root of
his irrational behavior and false expectations was his

pride. He felt he was entitled to be treated with respect and HE wanted to be the one to determine how that played out. He thought the water in the Jordan river was beneath his position and clout.

☕ LIFE APPLICATION

12. Can you think of a time when someone asked you to do more than you felt able to give? This could mean giving of your time, money, or even asking you to use a skill-set you didn't possess. How did you feel? What did you do?

Verse 13 of 2 Kings 5 reads: *Then his servants came near and spoke to him and said, "My father, had the prophet told you to do some great thing, would you not have done it? How much more then, when he says to you, 'Wash, and be clean?'"*

Sometimes we don't recognize that we even have expectations until we're faced with our own displeasure with a person or in a particular circumstance. You will face times when your expectations don't play out like the movie-script in your mind.

13. What is your typical reaction to disappointment?

If God asked you to do something significant, interesting, or important—something with apparent far-reaching impact for Him, would you do it? Hopefully, your answer is "yes." But how does the "yes" change when you approach the ordinary, seemingly small, daily interactions with those in your life whom you are called to love radically?

14. Here's a hypothetical situation: You are in a grocery store. All of the check-out lines are extremely long. (Even the express lines.) The people ahead of you all have a lot of items. You have only three things. You've had a busy day, and it's not over yet. Do you typically:

    a. Look at your watch, sigh, keep shifting your feet, and grow increasingly impatient with having to wait.
    b. Roll your eyes at the people in front of you who can't seem to get their act together, find their money, or load their groceries fast enough.
    c. Glare at everyone, hoping that if you stare hard enough someone will let you jump the line ahead of them.
    d. Ask if you can go ahead of someone else because you are "in a hurry."
    e. Wait patiently and take the opportunity to engage with those around you.

Have you ever left your grocery items right there on the magazine rack and walked away in a huff?

As you process your *typical* reaction to the above scenario, what are your expectations? What is your attitude?

15. Think about the parallel this makes to relationships. Is it possible to choose to walk away from important relationships because of expectations or inconvenience?

16. In the grocery store scenario, if you picked one of the choices of a., b., c., or d., what might happen if you waited patiently, took an interest in those around you, and even engaged someone in conversation?

JOURNAL
As you begin to examine your expectations, how
do you want God to help you?

CLOSING THOUGHTS

What if many of your relationship disappointments could
be avoided? What if healing and restoration of broken
relationships were possible? Loved one, if you were able to
tell us about the expectations you have on others, we could
help you avoid many future sorrows.

The last two verses of the 2 Kings 5 passage that we want
to show you read:

14 *So he went down and dipped himself in the Jordan,
according to the word of the man of God; and his flesh was
restored like the flesh of a little child and he was clean.* 15
*When he [Naaman] returned to the man of God with all his
company, and came and stood before him he said, "Behold
now, I know that there is no God in all the earth, but in
Israel."*

God doesn't conform to our expectations. In fact, most
often what God asks us to do will seem completely
backward to what we instinctively want to do. Thank
goodness for the counsel of wise friends without whom
Naaman would have chosen to cling to his expectations
and remain unhealed.

Think it's too late? Think you've already failed? Think
again! As you proceed through this study you can expect
this: God is going to give you many opportunities to
practice humility by doing the unexpected.

Nowhere in the Bible are we promised trouble-free relationships. In fact, we are told just the opposite. The Bible overflows with strategies to overcome conflicts. We can't promise that all of your relationships can be fully restored, but there is a miracle with your name on it. If you do things God's way your heart will be healed and you'll find you can have love for others, even when they don't love you back. That in itself is a huge miracle!

It begins by laying down your expectations. What if just by laying down your expectations you discovered many of your relationships were not as difficult as you imagined? We began this lesson by asking you to envision the great expectations that play out in your mind's eye. Through the story of Naaman we get a glimpse that God's ways are not our own, yet He always has our best interests in mind. Will you trust Him enough to tear up your script and allow His script to play out?

You can expect great things from God!

Session 2
Obedience

LESSON INTRODUCTION

Melanoma is one of the deadliest forms of skin cancer. More than 68,000 cases are diagnosed each year. It is one of the top six most common forms of cancer, and it is estimated that one person dies from melanoma every hour.

To catch melanoma early, it is recommended that everyone conduct a head-to-toe self-exam monthly. Melanoma is fairly easy to detect because it is easily visible on the skin. The death rate goes way up the longer melanoma goes unnoticed.

As important as it is to care for our bodies, it is even more important to engage in regular soul-searching, since that is the eternal part of our existence. The world has a way of making us sick. It turns our soft hearts into hearts of stone. It is easy to spot because it manifests in our rebellious attitudes and behaviors. However, early detection can greatly reduce the risk of faith-fatality.

When we speak to people about our book *Radical Love*, many ask, "What is it about?" We find with surprising consistency that when we tell them, the typical response is often, "Wow! I know someone who could really benefit from that message."

We all know "someone" who might benefit from a bold confrontation with truth from God's Word, don't we?

Honestly, it is a lot easier to believe God wants to work in someone else than to believe God wants each of us to do our own hard work of the soul.

It would grieve our hearts to know that someone walked away thinking only of the many others that should have read our book or done this study. *Examine Your Heart* is for you and we pray God uses some nugget from His Word to impact your heart forever from these pages.

Our first heart exam was about expectations. In this session, our heart-check is to take a look at our sacred calling as Christians. You have a calling, as do we. However, many miss it because it isn't what they were expecting.

The pastor is still looking for someone to help in children's church. A sick neighbor needs a ride to the cancer clinic. An elderly woman you know recently lost her sight and would love if someone would read to her each week. An unbelieving spouse is desperate for Jesus' help, but won't admit it. Difficult children need hours of extra attention. A co-worker is antagonistic about your Christian beliefs, but often asks you questions. A homeless man sits on the cold sidewalk near your office every day, with his hand held open.

Meanwhile, the Christian star-gazes wondering, "What is God's call on my life?" There are many frustrated believers looking for that specific plan. Loved one, God has strategically designed you to carry out a daring mission. It is no secret and it is found in Scripture. You are to love God and love the people God has placed in front of you. Yes, all of them.

That may sound rather ordinary. Perhaps even dreary and mundane. We've often allowed our culture to persuade our thinking. Maybe you've believed your calling should be huge—glamorous even. It certainly wasn't like that for Christ, was it? In the daily grind of life, God does His refining and perfecting work.

How, when, where, and with whom you live out your call will change. Sometimes in the blink of an eye. However, there will always be one common thread. 2 John 1:6 (NLT) sums it up perfectly: "Love means doing what God commands."

THE SPICY MEATBALL...
God's only call on your life is to be obedient to Him.

1. What is your reaction to this statement?

SCRIPTURE STUDY

It is nearly impossible to misinterpret what the Scriptures say when it comes to obedience to God's Word. The benefits are spelled out clearly. This is one area where the Word is straightforward. Dive into these verses with us and ask God to open your eyes to the importance He places on obedience. We think you'll see that everything else God has planned for you and everything He wants you to do on this exciting journey stems from your commitment to obey Him.

Matthew 22:35-40:
35 *One of them, a lawyer, asked Him [Jesus] a question, testing Him,* 36 *"Teacher, which is the greatest commandment in the Law?"*

37 *And He said to him, "'You shall love the Lord your God with all your heart, and with all your soul, and with all your mind.'* 38 *This is the greatest and foremost commandment.* 39 *The second is like it, 'You shall love your neighbor as yourself.'* 40 *On these two commandments depend the whole Law and the Prophets."*

2. What does Jesus say are the two greatest commandments?

3. What percentage of everything else in the Bible depend on these two commandments?

John 14:21:
21 *"He who has my commandments and keeps them is the one who loves Me; and he who loves me will be loved by My Father, and I will love him and will disclose Myself to him."*

4. There are two major benefits to keeping Jesus' commands listed in the above verse. What are they? Circle them.

John 15:12-14:
12 *"This is My commandment, that you love one another, just as I have loved you.* 13 *Greater love has no one than this, that one lay down his life for his friends.* 14 *You are my friends if you do what I have commanded you."*

5. What does a friend of Jesus do?

Do you want to be Jesus' friend? We do! Jesus' friends do what Jesus commands. Jesus commands that we love one another. The command to love and obey go hand-in-hand for a reason!

Deuteronomy chapter 11 provides a full listing of the benefits that come from obedience. It would be a worthwhile use of time to read it all and circle the promises within. Here is one verse that pulls it together nicely:

Deuteronomy 11:8:
8 *"You shall therefore keep every commandment which I am commanding you today, so that you may be strong and go in and possess the land into which you are about to cross to possess it;"*

6. Are we strengthened or weakened when we obey God's commands?

1 Corinthians 13 is an often quoted Scripture at weddings and anniversary celebrations of both Christians and non-Christians alike. Why? Because of the pure, selfless

description of love it depicts. But, dear friend, for a follower of Christ, these are not merely words of beautiful poetry, they are a detailed description of how we are to be one-to-another with **everyone**, not just a marriage relationship.

7. In the verses below circle all of the qualities of what love **is** with one color and what love is **not** in another.

If I speak with the tongues of men and of angels, but do not have love, I have become a noisy gong or a clanging cymbal. 2 If I have the gift of prophecy, and know all mysteries and all knowledge; and if I have all faith, so as to remove mountains, but do not have love, I am nothing. 3 And if I give all my possessions to feed the poor, and if I surrender my body to be burned, but do not have love, it profits me nothing.

4 Love is patient, love is kind and is not jealous; love does not brag and is not arrogant, 5 does not act unbecomingly; it does not seek its own, is not provoked, does not take into account a wrong suffered, 6 does not rejoice in unrighteousness, but rejoices with the truth; 7 bears all things, believes all things, hopes all things, endures all things.

8 Love never fails; but if there are gifts of prophecy, they will be done away; if there are tongues, they will cease; if there is knowledge, it will be done away. 9 For we know in part and we prophesy in part; 10 but when the perfect comes, the partial will be done away. 11 When I was a child, I used to speak like a child, think like a child, reason like a child; when I became a man, I did away with childish things. 12 For now we see in a mirror dimly, but then face to face; now I know in part, but then I will know fully just as I also have been fully known. 13 But now faith, hope, love, abide these three; but the greatest of these is love.

8. If you try and accomplish something—anything—
without displaying the qualities of love described in these
verses, what is the benefit?

 **LIFE APPLICATION**

In the Scripture study we learn that we are to love God and
love others.

9. As it stands right now, do you feel the Holy Spirit
nudging you more strongly in one or the other of these
commands? Which? Why?

10. Do you have an image in your mind of how a "good
Christian" would look and behave? What are those
characteristics?

11. Do you hold that image in your mind as the goal you strive towards?

12. Can someone exhibit the behaviors of a Christian without acting in true obedience to Jesus' commands? How?

13. "Obeying God all the time sounds miserable." Have you ever had this kind of thought? How would you respond if someone said this to you?

JOURNAL
Obedience is a word that puts people on the
defensive. Spend time talking / journaling
honestly to God about your feelings and behaviors
when it comes to obeying His commands.

CLOSING THOUGHTS

Rebellion. You can't turn on the T.V. or check out your news
feed without seeing hard evidence that hearts everywhere
are hardened toward any and all authority. The attitude is:
"I am my own boss and I don't have to listen to anyone; not
my parents, teacher, spouse, or even God."

What drives this rebellion? At the heart of rebellion is self-
centeredness and a lack of love. Can you see from this
session's study that loving others is a choice of obedience
and if you do not do it, there are hefty consequences?

Without love, Jesus will not disclose Himself to you. You are
not His friend. The Father will not know you. You are
nothing. Those are sobering words.

Don't be confused between choosing to demonstrate
Christ's love and "feeling" love for someone. We explore the
difference between the two more deeply as you continue
this study. There will be times when you don't feel like
doing the thing that you know you ought to do. When
choosing to show Christ's love seems to be the hardest
thing you've ever done, don't give up! Go to God and ask
Him for strength. Ask Him to show the love through you.
You won't always be able to love, but HE can.

Your purpose on earth is not a secret. Love God. Love
others. Use the gifts, talents, skills, personality, and other

wonderful qualities that God has given you to reach those who He places in your path with His love. It will be anything but boring. At the end of his life, do you think Paul looked back and thought about how mundane it was to follow Christ? How about those disciples? Can you imagine anyone, on his or her deathbed, looking back and regretting obedience to God?

Obedience to this call leads to success. Physically, emotionally, and especially, spiritually. Do you believe it?

Session 3
Salvation

LESSON INTRODUCTION

As we begin this lesson we'd like you to picture two scenarios:

First, have you ever shown up at a restaurant, thinking your reservation secure, only to be told, "We're sorry, we have no record of your name on our list?"

"But," you say, "I called months in advance and left a message." You show the manager the number you called.

"That isn't our number. I'm sorry. I can't help you. Your name isn't here. We don't have a place for you," the manager says, and you are ushered out.

That would be pretty frustrating, wouldn't it? You thought you did all the right things, but there was a missed step somewhere along the way.

Those of you with children may relate to this second scenario. Have you ever brought your children to an event, or perhaps a dinner at the home of someone you want to impress, like a boss or a new friend? Before you arrive at the destination, you may have a conversation that goes something like, "You better behave yourself in there. Use your manners, don't interrupt the adults talking, and no matter what food is served, say thank you and eat it!"

What you are asking your children to do is to manage their outward behaviors for a time period. You might even bribe them with a special treat if they behave for the duration of the time.

Sadly, our churches are filled with people who, for the most part, have been able to manage their outward behaviors without ever experiencing real heart change. We believe there is a horribly tragic deception that Satan has many church-goers under. The deception that they are saved, when in fact, they are not.

Even if you have been going to church for your entire life, it is possible that you are not saved. Why? Because going to church isn't what brings us into right relationship with God. "But," you might say, "I prayed a prayer of salvation when I was ____ years old!" Didn't that do the trick? Didn't that seal the deal? Hear us on this: Praying is certainly a part of the process. However, there is a critical component that many miss and the purpose of this session is to ensure you haven't missed it in your own life.

Metanoeo is the original Greek word from which our English word **repentance** is derived. It means to have a complete change when it comes to sin. Not just a change of mind—cause let's face it, it's easy to hate someone else's sin—but a complete change of emotional attachment to sin. Repentance happens when you see your sin the way God sees it—as disgusting! In light of that knowledge, repentance leads to a heartfelt sorrow which culminates in changing your behavior.

Jesus took the penalty of death for your sins. He paid the price. When you first recognize just how huge of a deal that is, the overwhelming sense of gratitude is the tinder to ignite a life-long passion to serve Him and to eradicate sin in your life with the help of the Holy Spirit. That initial realization is the first step. As you will see in this session, the decision to repent isn't a one-time occurrence. Repentance must happen any time God reveals your sin to you. It is the starting point for all godly change. Repentance keeps the communication lines open between you and God.

THE SPICY MEATBALL...
Many people who think they will spend eternity in heaven are actually going to be sent to hell.

1. What is your initial reaction to this statement? Does the thought make you shudder? Why or why not?

SCRIPTURE STUDY

Matthew 7:21-23:
21 *Not everyone who says to Me, "Lord, Lord," will enter the kingdom of heaven, but he who does the will of My Father who is in heaven will enter.* 22 *Many will say to Me on that day, "Lord, Lord, did we not prophesy in Your name, and in Your name cast out demons, and in Your name perform many miracles?"* 23 *And then I will declare to them, "I never knew you; depart from Me, you who practice lawlessness."*

2. In the above verses, Jesus is talking to His disciples. What is the quantity of people that will be sent away?

2 Corinthians 7:8-10:

8 *For though I caused you sorrow by my letter, I do not regret it; though I did regret it—for I see that that letter caused you sorrow, though only for a while— 9 I now rejoice, not that you were made sorrowful, but that you were made sorrowful to the point of repentance; for you were made sorrowful according to the will of God, so that you might not suffer loss in anything through us.*

10 *For the sorrow that is according to the will of God produces a repentance without regret, leading to salvation, but the sorrow of the world produces death.*

3. What caused the Corinthians sorrow?

4. What is God's will regarding sorrow?

5. What does repentance lead to?

6. From these verses, does it appear that one can be sorrowful and <u>not</u> receive salvation? Explain.

Acts 2:37-38:
*37 Now when they heard this, they were pierced to the heart,
and said to Peter and the rest of the apostles, "Bretheren,
what shall we do?"*

*38 Peter said to them, "Repent, and each of you be baptized
in the name of Jesus Christ for the forgiveness of your sins;
and you will receive the gift of the Holy Spirit."*

7. Leading up to verse 37, Peter had disclosed the truth
about Jesus to the Israelites. These were the very people
who supported Jesus' crucifixtion. When they heard the
truth about their sin, about what they did and to whom
they did it, how were they affected?

8. What did Peter tell them to do about their realization
that they'd done wrong?

Notice, these people were affected when they heard who
Jesus really was. They were pierced to the heart! This is an
emotional reaction. But that wasn't enough to give them
the gift of the Holy Spirit. Peter told them what had to
happen next, and it began with repentance.

LIFE APPLICATION

9. Both Paul and Peter confronted other people about their sin. When you are confronted with a sin you've committed (confronted either by another person or by the Holy Spirit convicting your heart) what is your typical reaction?

10. Is there something in your life in which you are continually sorry for the outcome, but when given the opportunity, you do it again?

Dear friend, question 10 may be very difficult for you to address. If you are sorry for the outcome of a sinful action, but you want to continue to do it, then you have not repented of the behavior.

In chapter 3 of *Radical Love*, we take a very close look at the life of Peter. We compare his behaviors before he received the Holy Spirit and after. Before, he was fearful and when given the opportunity he denied knowing Jesus. After, he couldn't stop preaching about the truth of Jesus as savior of the world. He preached right up until he was martyred for his Lord. The Holy Spirit brought about a change of life, change of heart, and change of behaviors. Peter couldn't stop talking about Jesus because the entire ministry of the Holy Spirit is to testify about the truth of Christ.

11. Up to this point, did you fully understand the critical role the Holy Spirit has in salvation?

12. What were the circumstances leading up to your salvation?

JOURNAL
Like Peter, are there marked differences in you from before your salvation and after? What are they? In what areas is God still calling you to repent?

CLOSING THOUGHTS

Belief that Jesus is God's Son and was crucified for your sin
is a portion of your salvation. Yes, you must embrace His
death and resurrection as the reason you can be in right
standing with God. However, if you know this, but have no
change in how you feel about your personal sins... if you
continue to willingly give sin top spot in your life... if you
have not been made sorrowful to the point of repentance as
it relates to your sin, then you have not been saved. The
Holy Spirit is not a part of the Christian life, He is so critical
we would say that without Him, the Christian has no life.

It is process. You won't get it right every time. Old habits will
surface. Unloving words will come forth from your own lips.
However, you will notice in increasing measures you are
able to put into practice that which God teaches you. If you
desire God to refine you, then ask Him to do it! He will. Ask
Him to help you hate your sinful ways. Ask Him to help you
respond with His love. Pursue Him and He will disclose
Himself more and more to you. There is an awesome
promise found in Philippians 2:13: "For God is working in
you, to give you the desire and the power to do what pleases
Him." (NLT)

Because you are on this journey, we feel confident that you
don't want to be one of the *many* who expect to feast at the
banquet in heaven, only to be told there is no record of your
name. We want to leave you with one last question to
examine your heart in regards to your salvation:
Have you had the moment of realization of just how ugly
your sin is to God or are you managing your outward
behavior with no inner change?

Session 4
Motives

LESSON INTRODUCTION

Betty White turned 93 years old on January 17, 2015.
There is a television commercial that features Betty White
playing football with a bunch of twenty-something year old
men. She can't keep up. She gets tackled into the mud. The
team gets on her case for playing weakly and they give her
a Snickers candy bar. After she eats the Snickers, she
transforms into a young guy who's got his game back. She's
got her strength.

The tagline for Snickers: **Snickers satisfies**.

When it comes to your Christian faith, do you at times feel
like Betty White on the football field? Weak, not up to
speed with the rest of the Christians, unable to do what's
required in the heat of the moment?

Jesus has instructed us to love others in the way He loves:
Sacrificial, selfless, others-centered love. Unfortunately,
this kind of love is not what Satan would like us to give. It
goes against our sinful natures. Satan wants us to be
selfish, focused on ourselves, looking out for our own best
interests at all costs. As such, many are deceived into
thinking sex, love, and intimacy are one and the same.

When your ideas about love come from what you see
anywhere but God's word, you are going to form
expecations that God does not intend you to have. Where

do these expectations come from?

- Believing the fairy-tale love ideology presented in chick-flicks, Disney movies, or other romantic comedies;
- Acceptance to the idea that we cannot control our sexual orientation or whom we fall in love with;
- Giving in to the temptation to view pornography, including lingering on images in swimsuit calendars, lingerie ads, fireman (male model) calendars;
- Reading fiction books that ooze with sexual scenarios—like *Fifty Shades of Grey* or other erotica books.

Notice this: you can control what you believe to be true about love. You decide what you pay attention to. You can decide what you read. You decide what you look at on the internet. You decide what you "feed" your mind with. When you feed it with anything but what God says about love, you will remain Betty White when it comes to having the strength to love when things get tough.

The expectation for self-seeking love is not limited to a marriage relationship. Every aspect of worldly love puts you at the center. It seeps into what you seek from your family, children, friendships—even your relationship with God. How many times have you heard it said, "God wants me to be happy"? The quest for this love is self-idolatry! It is a great tragedy to believe that what the world teaches about love is true love.

The Bible contains ALL of the necessary strategies for loving others unconditionally. We must believe in the Bible's sufficiency in this area. The power to follow through comes from the Holy Spirit. He brings the love and He can overcome any barrier or false expectation you may have formed about love. He can equip you mightily to love others in a radically different way: Christ's way! It begins when you seek to view others with the same mindset that Christ has when He views us. Let's start by satisfying our hunger with God's Word to learn what the Bible reveals about Christ's love.

THE SPICY MEATBALL...
If you choose not to love someone with Christ's mindset, you choose to side with Satan.

1. What is your initial reaction to this statement?

SCRIPTURE STUDY

If you are going to love with Christ's mindset, you must first understand what choices Christ made and why.

Philippians 2:3-4:
3 *Do nothing from selfishness or empty conceit, but with humility of mind, regard one another as more important than yourselves; 4 do not merely look out for your own personal interests, but also for the interests of others.*

2. This passage was written to believers in Christ. As a believer, how does this passage say you are to regard others?

3. What does Paul say is acceptable for us to do selfishly?

Continue reading Philippians 2:5-8:

5 Have this attitude in yourselves which was also in Christ Jesus, 6 who, although He existed in the form of God, did not regard equality with God a thing to be grasped, 7 but emptied Himself, taking the form of a bond-servant, and being made in the likeness of men. 8 Being found in appearance as a man, He humbled Himself by becoming obedient to the point of death, even death on a cross.

4. In the verses above, circle or highlight the choices Christ made.

Continue reading Philippians 2:9-15:

9 For this reason also, God highy exalted Him, and bestowed on Him the name which is above every name, 10 so that at the name of Jesus EVERY KNEE WILL BOW, of those who are in heaven and on earth and under the earth, 11 and that every tongue will confess that Jesus Christ is Lord, to the glory of God the Father.

12 So then, my beloved, just as you have always obeyed, not as in my presence only, but now much more in my absence, work out your salvation with fear and trembling; 13 for it is God who is at work in you, both to will and to work for His good pleasure.

14 Do all things without grumbling or disputing; 15 so that you will prove yourselves to be blameless and innocent, children of God above reproach in the midst of a crooked and perverse generation, among whom you appear as lights in the world...

5. According to verse 11, why did Christ make the choices He made?

6. Why is it important that we act in the way listed in these verses? (see verse 15)

7. To emphasize the point, when you do not show yourself as a child of God in this world, whose efforts are you supporting?

Matthew 16:21-23:
21 *From that time, Jesus began to show His disciples that He must go to Jerusalem, and suffer many things from the elders and chief priests and scribes, and be killed, and be raised up on the third day. 22 Peter took Him aside and began to rebuke Him, saying, "God forbid it, Lord! This shall never happen to You."*

23 *But He turned and said to Peter, "Get behind Me, Satan! You are a stumbling block to Me; for you are not setting your mind on God's interests, but man's."*

8. Because Peter's mind was not focused on God's interests, what does Jesus call him?

Each time you intentionally decide to do something your way, not God's way, you support Satan's efforts in that moment.

LIFE APPLICATION

Your mind, set on God's interests, means you are removed from the center of your pursuits. Have you heard or used any of the following statements:

"You need to do what you feel is right."

"If it makes you happy, then do it."

"I'm through with him (or her)!"

"I've got to look out for myself."

9. Whose interests are at the center of these kinds of statements?

10. How would you re-word the statements to put Christ at the center?

Often, when we teach on this topic, we have at least one person come to us and say, "So you are telling me that I should let people act however they want and not say anything about it? Should I just give in to everyone's demands, no matter what?"

No. That is completely not what we are saying. If your child wanted to eat nothing but candy, obviously that would not be in his or her best interest, even though it would make your child feel good (for a while, anyway). When you put someone else's interests ahead of your own, it can be extremely difficult. The easiest way out is not necessarily God's answer.

Do you realize that when you have the Holy Spirit, you have access to Christ's mind in any situation? It's true. 1 Corinthians 2:16 says, "But we have the mind of Christ."

Each scenario is different. Every person is unique. And Christ knows what is needed to show God's glory and He alone knows what is in the best interests of that individual person. Your job? To be willing and obedient to what He asks.

11. Are there people in your life who you think are not deserving of your self-sacrifice? Who are they and why do you feel this way about them?

12. Moving forward, what kinds of situations do you envision will be difficult for you to demonstrate Christ's love? What can you do to be equipped in those situations?

JOURNAL

What is one small step today that you can take with one of those difficult people that would show them Christ-minded love? Spend time picturing those tough scenarios. Write how you feel and commit your future responses to God.

CLOSING THOUGHTS

Your prior expectations and beliefs about love are influenced by a combination of variables. Past experiences, media, culture, peers, and prior understanding of God's love all contribute to how you manage your relationships. When God shows you that you need to give grace to someone who you "feel" doesn't deserve it, you need a strategy for handling things. Your first reaction will be what we call a "Yeah, but..."

"Yeah, but God, she hurt my feelings."

"Yeah, but God, I am right and he is wrong."
"Yeah, but God, I don't have time to deal with this."
"Yeah, but God, he has wounded me deeply."

We all have our "yeah, buts." Here's a truth: God has no
"yeah, but" when it comes to whether or not someone
deserves His grace. Every "yeah, but" you give is like adding
a brick to a wall that will cut you off from hearing from God
in the matter. Stop the "yeah, buts" and you'll hear more
from God. It's that simple. Notice, we didn't say it was "easy,"
but the process is simple. Let go of your own expectation
and follow through with what is in the best spiritual interest
of the person you need to love.

Session 5 Trust

LESSON INTRODUCTION

Have you ever played the opposite game? Kids love this game. You say a word and the other person comes up with its opposite. Here's a question: What's the opposite of trusting God? Ask that question to 10 people and the majority will reply, "doubting God." We'd like you to shift your thinking a bit by saying that the opposite of trusting God is **trusting man**.

Two things that throw up a roadblock to trusting God are pride and despair. Pride says, "I can do it myself. I don't need God." Despair declares, "God is not big enough for my problem and doesn't care about me." Often, when we have a problem loving others, our mindset goes to one or the other.

When we are prideful, we think we know how to handle a situation in the best way. You might pray to God, but you go forward full speed with your own plans. And, if the Holy Spirit nudges you in a way that you don't like, you'll make an excuse as to why that way won't work.

Desperation drives us to grasp at any and every strategy that is presented before us. A local radio station has a segment called "Help Me Fridays." Every Friday, listeners have the chance to call in with their relationship problems, then other listeners respond by phoning in their advice. As you can imagine, if 50 people call in, the person with the problem has 50 different opinions on what he or she should do.

Often, we'll try every solution man can think of rather than tackling a matter God's way. Why? Because when push comes to shove we don't trust that God's way of handling a matter will be the outcome *we* want it to be.

In this session, we look at what "trusting God" means on a practical, day to day level. When it comes to loving others, you simply must trust God. Your own plans, the plans you get from friends, or the pop-culture self-help gurus may or may not work. It's hit or miss. But God's way is always right.

Trusting God manifests itself in different ways:
- Obeying the straightforward commands of the Bible
- Praying to God in your time of need
- Seeking what the Bible instructs when you need clarity on a matter
- Gaining counsel from a godly source
- Commitment to follow through, even if things are hard

Your trust should not be placed in the hopes for a desired outcome; even though God knows your heart's desires. Your first trust is in the character and the fulfillment of the promises of God. His way will always provide the best outcome. Always!

Trusting God takes practice. Quieting the voices of the masses to hear God's voice takes practice. Your entire faith life hinges on your ability to trust God. You can do it, one decision at a time.

THE SPICY MEATBALL...
Whenever you try and control the outcome of a situation, you do not trust God.

1. Do you agree with this statement? Why or why not?

SCRIPTURE STUDY

Today we travel to the Old Testament to study the action that took place immediately prior to the Israelites' forty year period of wandering the desert. We see how and why they were given that punishment from God, and how it could have been avoided.

Numbers 13:1-2: (NIV)
1 *The LORD said to Moses,* 2 *"Send some men to explore the land of Canaan, which I am giving the Israelites. From each ancestral tribe send one of its leaders."*

2. What the purpose of the mission?

3. How many leaders were sent on this mission?

It was common practice to survey the land prior to moving into battle. Before we assess the outcome of the story, you cannot miss the fact that the purpose of the mission was not to determine whether or not they **should** take the land. They were to explore and plan **how** to move in and take that which God already promised. Let's see what happens:

Numbers 13:27-30:
27 *They gave Moses this account: "We went into the land to which you sent us, and it does flow with milk and honey: here is its fruit. 28 But the people who live there are powerful, and the cities are fortified and very large. We even saw descendents of Anak there. 29 The Amalekites live in the Negev; the Hittites, Jebusites, and Amorites live in the hill country; and the Canaanites live near the sea and along the Jordan."*

30 *Then Caleb silenced the people before Moses and said, "We should go up and take possession of the land, for we can certainly do it." 31 But the men who had gone up with him said, "We can't attack those people; they are stronger than we are." 32 And they spread among the Israelites a bad report about the land they had explored. They said, "The land we explored devours those living in it. All the people we saw there are of great size."*

4. The 12 scouts came back with a report about the people in the land. Did all of the men have the same opinion regarding what should be done? Who reported differently?

5. What was it about the enemies that made the other Israelites think they would not win in a battle against them?

A little further in this passage we see how God responds to this report and the subsequent actions taken by the Israelites. First, let's see how Caleb and his friend Joshua try to change the people's minds:

Numbers 14:6-14:
6 *Joshua, son of Nun, and Caleb, son of Japhunneh, who were*
among those who had explored the land tore their clothes 7
and said to the entire Israelites assembly, "The land we
passed through and explored is exceedingly good. 8 *If the*
LORD is pleased with us, He will lead us into that land, a land
flowing with milk and honey, and will give it to us. 9 *Only do*
not rebel against the LORD. And do not be afraid of the
people of the land, because He will swallow them up. Their
protection is gone, but the LORD is with us. Do not be afraid
of them."

10 *But the whole assembly talked about stoning them. Then*
the glory of the LORD appeared at the Tent of the Meeting to
all the Israelites. 11 *The LORD said to Moses, "How long will*
these people treat me with contempt? How long will they
refuse to believe Me, in spite of all the miraculous signs I
have performed among them?"

6. By refusing to go into the land, who did Caleb and Joshua
tell the people that they were rebelling against?

7. What was the primary emotion that kept the Israelites
from wanting to go into the land and take it?

8. Their fear was so extreme, what did they talk about
doing to the two men who wanted to obey the LORD?

9. In verse 11, highlight how the LORD said the people were treating Him. Also highlight what the LORD said the people were refusing to do.

When you have contempt for someone, you do not give him any honor. You treat him with disgust, disregard, anger. That is how God said the people treated Him when they refused to do things His way. The consequences for their disobedience were great. In these verses, God is speaking:

Numbers 14:22-24: (NIV)
22 *"Not one of the men who saw my glory and the miraculous signs I performed in Egypt and in the desert but who disobeyed Me and tested Me ten times,* 23 *not one of them will ever see the land I promised on oath to their forefathers. No one who has treated me with contempt will ever see it.* 24 *But because my servant Caleb has a different spirit and follows me wholeheartedly, I will bring him into the land he went to, and his descendants will inherit it."*

10. Did those who disobeyed get to enjoy the blessing of the Promised Land?

11. Why was Caleb spared? What does it say exactly?

LIFE APPLICATION

There are so many applications in this passage!

12. What areas of your life—or in what kinds of problems you face—do you make self-preserving decisions at the expense of handling the matter God's way? Another way to ask it is: In which situations do you try and maintain control over an outcome?

13. Do you think your attempt to maintain control is driven by fear?

14. How does it make you feel to think that when you do not trust God, He could look upon you and say the same as He did to the Israelites: "You are treating Me with contempt"?

JOURNAL

When fear comes upon you, you have a decision to make. How you respond will be determined by your pursuit of God when things are going well. What can you begin to do **today** that will prepare you for those moments when you are tempted to look to the world's answers instead of trusting God's way?

CLOSING THOUGHTS

When you say to God, "I trust You," it is critical to understand what it is that you are trusting. You trust God when you seek to handle a matter His way. You trust that the outcome will be in the best interests for all involved. It does not necessarily mean that other people will do what you want them to do. That is so important for you to understand. You may have plans or hopes for a desired outcome; but when it doesn't happen the way you want it, you must rely on God that He will show you the next steps and that He will carry you through the matter.

Every act of faith is rewarded. Caleb and Joshua were the only two of those Israelites who got to enter God's Promised Land; His place of blessing. The others brought their own destruction upon themselves by not only mistrusting God, but by getting so fearful that they wanted to stone God's servants!

In question 11 of this session, we hope you notice that God said that Caleb was spared because he had a "different spirit" than the others. Like Caleb, if you have been saved, you have a different spirit, too. The Holy Spirit.

Caleb and Joshua placed their trust in the promise of success that God gave them. God has made some promises to you. Lots of them, actually. God promises:

- To supply for every need you have. (Phil. 4:19)
- That His grace is sufficient for you. (2 Cor. 12:9)
- That His children will always be able to escape temptation to sin. (1 Cor. 10:13 & Jude 1:24)
- That all things (no matter how they appear to our human minds) will work together for good for those who love Him. (Rom. 8:28)

These are just 4 of them. The Bible is FULL of promises you can cling to for any situation you will face. Resist the temptation to take matters into your own hands. You will need to take action—the Israelites would have had to step out and engage in the battle against their enemies in order to see God's mighty hand save them—but you must ensure the action you take is handling things God's way.
Psalm 32:10 (NIV) reads: *"Many are the woes of the*

wicked—but the LORD'S unfailing love surrounds the man who trusts in Him."

Do we hear an, "Amen!"?

Session 6
Temper

LESSON INTRODUCTION

The leader went away. He had been summoned to a
meeting with his boss. He told the people he'd be back; but
he wasn't sure when. The people thought he'd be right
back. When a day went by, and then two, and then more,
they began to wonder what happened. "Is he ever coming
back?" "Has something happened to him?" "What if he's
dead?" The questions worried them. Fear consumed them.
As days passed they forgot the things the leader taught
them about how they were to live and the guidelines he
had given. They began to look to each other for answers
when problems arose. They began to make up their own
rules. Eventually, they forgot about the leader altogether.
When he finally returned, he barely recognized the people
in his charge.

This is what happened when Moses went up Mount Sinai
to meet with God (as told in Exodus). The Israelites did not
stay faithful. Moses didn't return when they thought he
should return and they abandoned the things they knew
about God. They didn't turn from God the moment Moses
left. It happened over time. One decision led to another...
they drifted.

Our modern culture offers us many opportunities to be
fickle with our faith if we aren't careful. People, things, and
ideals catch our attention and if we linger there too long,

we begin to drift toward those things and away from God.
Whereas there are many things that can fall into this
category, in this session we are going to dig deep into
something that can not only cause you to drift from your
faith, but abandon it altogether: jealousy.

THE SPICY MEATBALL...
Harboring feelings of envy can eventually lead
you to abandon your faith.

1. Do you agree with this statement? Why or why not?

As the church of Corinth grew, they allowed the culture
around them to influence them. Paul rebuked them sharply
in his epistle (1 Corinthians). We can picture him yelling at
them: "Grow up! You are acting just like children who don't
know how to behave!" He was greatly disturbed when he
wrote, *"I can no longer speak to you as spiritual men... For
since there is jealousy and strife among you, are you not
fleshly, and are you not walking like mere men?"* (1
Corinthians 1 & 3)

Paul's words pack a punch that should be felt by anyone
ready to give in to the temptation to be jealous. Satan will
use the things around you to tell you that everyone else has
what you deserve. How do you avoid the temptation to

believe it?

Knowing how to quickly identify jealousy and deal with it is critical to loving radically. When not dealt with, jealousy turns to bitterness, then anger, and rage. Allowing envy to seep into any part of your heart and stay there is a first step in drifting from your faith. Let's examine our tempers and fight the green-eyed monster where it hurts him most: in God's Word.

SCRIPTURE STUDY

Genesis 4 contains the story of the first murder committed on earth. Two brothers. Cain and Abel. As we study this event we will examine the choices Cain made, his mood, and what actions he took. We'll see that Cain's circumstance was not unlike situations we face every day.

Genesis 4:3-8:
3 *In the course of time Cain brought some of the fruits of the soil as an offering to the LORD. 4 But Abel brought fat portions from some of the firstborn of his flock. The LORD looked with favor on Abel and his offering, 5 but on Cain and his offering he did not look with favor. So Cain was very angry, and his face was downcast.*

6 *Then the LORD said to Cain, "Why are you angry? Why is your face downcast? 7 If you do what is right, will you not be accepted? But if you do not do what is right, sin is crouching at your door; it desires to have you, but you must master it.*

8 *Now Cain said to his brother Abel, "Let's go out into the field." And while they were in the field, Cain attacked his brother Abel and killed him.*

2. God showed favor on Abel, but not on Cain. Regardless of whether Cain's offering was less acceptable because he didn't follow God's instructions, or Cain's heart wasn't right when he made the offering, the end result was that God deemed it unfavorable. At the end of verse 5, how does Cain feel?

3. What does the LORD ask Cain in verse 6? Highlight it.

4. Why do you think Cain was angry?

Oh the Life Application is going to be good on this one! In the Life Application of session 3 (question 9 on page 32) we asked you to examine your reaction when you are confronted by sin. Look back at your answer. Do you repent quickly? Or do you get angry, frustrated, mad that you were caught? Our human nature is to hate it when we're busted doing something we shouldn't have done. We are creatures of temper! Cain was no different. He was busted. And God gave him a choice at that point.

5. What choice did God give Cain?

6. What warning did God give Cain?

Follow the process here: Cain saw that his brother had something that he did not: God's favor. He became angry. God called him out on his anger and gave him a chance to repent.

7. Did Cain repent at that point? What choice did Cain make?

Let's read on...

Genesis 4:9-10:
9 *Then the LORD said to Cain, "Where is your brother Abel?" "I don't know," he replied. "Am I my brother's keeper?"*

10 *Then the LORD said, "What have you done? Listen! Your brother's blood cries out to me from the ground."*

8. Did God know what Cain had done?

9. If God already knew Abel was dead, why do you think He asked the question of Cain?

Let's continue...

Genesis 4:11-16:

11 *Now you are under a curse and driven from the ground,
which opened its mouth to receive your brother's blood from
your hand.* 12 *When you work the ground, it will no longer
yield its crops for you. You will be a restless wanderer on the
earth.*

13 *Cain said to the LORD, "My punishment is more than I can
bear.* 14 *Today you are driving me from the land, and I will
be hidden from your presence; I will be a restless wanderer
on the earth, and whoever finds me will kill me."*

15 *But the LORD said, "Not so; if anyone kills Cain, he will
suffer vengeance seven times over." Then the LORD put a
mark on Cain so that no one who found him would kill him.*
16 *So Cain went out from the LORD's presence and lived in
the land of Nod, east of Eden.*

10. When Cain repeats his punishment in verse 14 is it the
same as what the Lord said? What is different?

11. Did the LORD ever tell Cain that Cain would be
"hidden" from the LORD's presence? What are the first two
words that God said to Cain in verse 15?

12. Who left who in verse 16?

Let's track the action again: Cain saw that his brother had something that he did not: God's favor. He became angry. God called him out on his anger and gave him a chance to repent. He did not. He killed his brother. God gave him another chance to repent. He did not. God told him what his consequence was for his sin. Cain still did not repent. Even then, God put a mark of protection on Cain. Cain left the LORD's presence.

LIFE APPLICATION

13. What does the phrase: "He/She has a bad temper" mean to you?

14. Right from the beginning, the LORD gave Cain a stern warning against hanging on to his anger. Is there a time when you knew you were hanging on to anger even though your spirit was being prompted to do differently? What ended up happening?

JOURNAL

Who do you envy? What do you covet?
Has God warned you against this? What do you do when you feel jealousy arise?

CLOSING THOUGHTS

Where your eyes linger too long are the places where Satan is going to tempt you with jealousy which can lead to anger. He will tempt you to be angry because you don't have what someone else has. Your anger will be directed at the person you blame for not having that thing. Your anger may even be directed at God for not "blessing" you in the way He's blessed someone else. When you feel anger, you must speak it out to God and allow Him to instruct you.

In Hebrews 11:4 we are told that Abel made a better sacrifice than Cain. But Cain's falter in this area didn't discredit him from God's mercy. The point we want you to see is what Cain did with his mistake. When God blessed someone else, Cain let envy and anger lead him to sin.

It will always be a temptation to compare yourself and your life to others. Our media-rich environment bombards us with things we "must" have. If you look hard enough you can find someone who appears prettier, skinnier, smarter, more handsome, has a better spouse, bigger house, and who drives a nicer car. Always. Within the church, you will hear stories of God using other people in mighty ways. God doing the miraculous for other families. God providing for somebody else. You may feel envious that you are not a part of it; especially if you are doing your very best to follow after God wholeheartedly.

Unless you take those feelings to God when they surface, there is great danger that they will create a barrier between you and the Holy Spirit. Cain held onto his anger. He refused to calm it. He didn't change his thought pattern and the anger led him to a rage that caused sin. Murder! But even then God gave him a chance to repent.

Cain left God's presence. In reality, there is nowhere on earth that is out of God's presence. But you can sure choose

to ignore Him. You can allow envy, anger, and sinful blame
to block the voice of the Holy Spirit. You can choose
mindless entertainment over connecting with Him. It is a
wonderful, freeing truth to know that God will always
present you with a choice when you are faced with
temptation.

Proverbs 21:16 reads: *"A man who wanders from the way of
understanding will rest in the assembly of the dead."*

Yikes! Don't let your eyes wander. Don't let your faith
wander. God will always have a solution for you.

Session 7
Mercy

LESSON INTRODUCTION

Humans love to pick sides. When you go to a wedding, you sit on the left (bride's side) or the right (groom's side). When you go to a sporting event, you root for the home team or the away team. Politically you lump yourself in as a liberal or conservative. You are pro-life or pro-choice.

Have you ever considered that every person on earth is in one of two categories: they are going to heaven when they die or they are going to hell. You are on God's team or you are on Satan's team.

In many areas you can "sit the fence." You can declare no political allegiance and remain neutral. Sure, you can go to a football game and truly have no care who wins. You can love both the bride and the groom equally. But hear this: There is no neutral zone when it comes to Jesus. You either know Him as your LORD and Savior or you do not. If you died this minute, you will hear, "Welcome, good and faithful servant," or you will hear, "Depart from Me, I never knew you."

Pause a moment and consider the implications of that. What would you hear if you were to die right now? Are you sure? In session 3 we talked about a key component to your salvation: repentance. Confession is the best friend of repentance. Confession is the fuse that lights the dynamite to blow up the barrier and return you to right standing with God.

Have you ever told a child to "say sorry" to a sibling for something that was done wrong. The child blurts out a sarcastic, "Sorry," to which you have to reply, "OK, now say it again and mean it!"

Saying sorry and being sorry are two different things. In our homes, when a person says sorry, we've instilled the practice of declaring what the person is sorry for. Specifically.

"I'm sorry I pulled the arms off of your Barbie doll and taped them to my toy dinosaur."

"I'm sorry I came home in a bad mood and took it out on you."

"I'm sorry for being selfish."

"I'm sorry for using ugly words."

Kids and adults alike need to be in the habit of not just saying sorry, but truly *being* sorry. Then, we must do our part to put our sorry into action. Make a change. Make it right.

When you confess your sins to God, He sees the heart condition. He knows if you mean your "sorry." When your heart condition is right, your sins are forgiven. Jesus tells us that just as we are forgiven, we are to forgive those who wrong us. In this session you will examine your heart to identify the amount of mercy you are prepared to show others. All unforgiveness must be confessed to God. A battle rages in the heart of every believer. The double-mind of the heart is this: whether to surrender to the temptation to sin or to press on, striving for purity.

Sooner or later all decide which master they will serve: God or Satan. Unforgiveness toward others gives Satan supremacy over your life. To forgive another is to bow before a Holy God. The best news of all is YOU get to decide which master you will serve. This is the free will that God has given you.

You either know or you don't know the magnitude of the cost for your own forgiveness. Your heart can accept, rejoice, and respond in gratitude for the freedom that comes with forgiveness or it can harden, deny, and even reject God's forgiveness altogether.

THE SPICY MEATBALL...
If you do not demonstrate forgiveness to others in increasing measure, Jesus will not forgive you.

1. How does the above statement make you feel? Are there things that could happen that you don't think you would forgive?

SCRIPTURE STUDY

Matthew 18:21-35:

21 *Then Peter came and said to Him, "Lord, how often shall my brother sin against me and I forgive him? Up to seven times?" 22 Jesus said to him, "I do not say to you, up to seven times, but up to seventy times seven.*

23 *For this reason the kingdom of heaven may be compared to a king who wished to settle accounts with his slaves. 24 When he had begun to settle them, one who owed him ten thousand talents was brought to him. 25 But since he did not have the means to repay, his lord commanded him to be sold, along with his wife and children and all that he had, and repayment to be made.*

26 *So the slave fell to the ground and prostrated himself before him, saying, 'Have patience with me and I will repay you everything.' 27 And the lord of that slave felt compassion and released him and forgave him the debt.*

28 *But that slave went out and found one of his fellow slaves who owed him a hundred denarii; and he seized him and began to choke him, saying, 'Pay back what you owe.' 29 So his fellow slave fell to the ground and began to plead with him, saying, 'Have patience with me and I will repay you.' 30 But he was unwilling and went and threw him in prison until he should pay back what was owed.*

31 *So when his fellow slaves saw what had happened, they were deeply grieved and came and reported to their lord all that had happened.*

32 *Then summoning him, his lord said to him, 'You wicked slave, I forgave you all that debt because you pleaded with me. 33 Should you not also have had mercy on your fellow slave, in the same way that I had mercy on you?' 34 And his*

lord, moved with anger, handed him over to the torturers until he should repay all that was owed him.

35 *My heavenly Father will also do the same to you, if each of you does not forgive his brother from your heart."*

2. What was Peter's question in verse 21?

3. In response, Jesus tells a parable. What does Jesus say this parable is about? (verse 23)

4. The king and the slave demonstrate very different responses when each is presented with the opportunity to forgive. In the chart below, list how each responded when asked for forgiveness:

KING   **SLAVE**

5. Who witnessed the slave's demonstration of unforgiveness? What emotion did they feel and what did they do about it?

6. What was the outcome for the unforgiving slave?

7. What is Jesus' warning in verse 35? Highlight where the forgiveness is to come from.

Mark 11:25

25 "*Whenever you stand praying, forgive, if you have anything against anyone, so that your Father who is in heaven will also forgive you your transgressions.*"

8. Who and what does Jesus say we should forgive?

9. Highlight in verse 25 WHY we should forgive?

Often, we hesitate to forgive because we feel like if we do, we are letting the other person "get away with" something. Friend, we hope you notice that the forgiveness isn't for them, Jesus says it is for YOU!

Titus 3:1-7:

1 *Remind them to be subject to rulers, to authorities, to be obedient, to be ready for every good deed,* 2 *to malign no one, to be peaceable, gentle, showing every consideration for all men.* 3 *For we also once were foolish ourselves, disobedient, deceived, enslaved to various lusts and pleasures, spending our life in malice and envy, hateful, hating one another.*

4 *But when the kindness of God our Savior and His love for mankind appeared,* 5 *He saved us, not on the basis of deeds which we have done in righteousness, but according to His mercy, by the washing of regeneration and renewing by the Holy Spirit,* 6 *whom He poured out upon us richly through Jesus Christ our Savior,* 7 *so that being justified by His grace we would be made heirs according to the hope of eternal life.*

10. According to verse 5 above, why did God save us?

11. Verse 1 above reads that we are "to be ready for every good deed." Do you think this includes being ready to forgive? Explain.

12. In light of our salvation, how are we to treat others? Circle in verse 2 each instruction given.

You are to remember: You, too, were once far from God. His mercy allows you to come close.

LIFE APPLICATION

13. In light of all you've read throughout this session's study, how would you answer if Peter had asked you, "How many times must I forgive an offense against me?"

14. How would you answer the question: "What if someone doesn't say they are sorry? Should I forgive them?"

15. Is there an offense that you believe is too great to forgive? Explain.

JOURNAL

This is a difficult question, but one that must be asked. Do you currently hold something against someone else? Are you withholding mercy? What are you going to do to move forward?

CLOSING THOUGHTS

Throughout this lesson, you may have felt like something was stabbing at you, the way a woodpecker pokes at a tree. That nagging feeling is the Holy Spirit, wanting you to perk up and take notice because there is someone you need to forgive.

Remember, God isn't concerned with outward appearances. He is so incredible, He can look right into your heart and see its condition. You may or may not have to go to the person who needs your forgiveness; but you can ask God right now to make your heart right in the matter. God knows if you truly desire to be merciful toward that person.

How can you tell if your heart is right? How do you know when you are free from the burden of unforgiveness? When you can look upon someone who has wronged you and feel **compassion** for them. It is a process and may require you to continue to ask God to soften your heart when Satan is nudging and reminding you that you were wronged. Avoid the temptation to replay the offense in your mind. That is 100% from Satan. One day, you will realize that you no longer want to bring up the past hurt again. Freedom!

It is because you have a different spirit—the Holy Spirit—that you are able to forgive all offenses, great or small. If you try and forgive in your own power, there will always be a breaking point. Without Christ, there will always be an unforgivable offense.

Jesus' point in the parable we studied was that once you realize the depth of your own forgiveness, you absolutely cannot hold any debt against anyone else for any reason. He's got the right to make that claim, don't you think? If you doubt it picture Him hanging, bloody and beaten beyond recogniztion on the cross. Picture Him looking at you and declaring, "This is for YOUR offenses."

Now, we ask again, picture the person who has wronged you. Can you ask God to help you forgive them?

Session 8
Love

LESSON INTRODUCTION

We enter into this last session coming back to the small word with big power: **love**.

Each heart-check we've done along the way in regards to your expectations, obedience, salvation, motives, trust, temper, and mercy is a piece of the puzzle when it comes to giving Christ's complete and perfect love to those around you.

Each life application question, each suggestion for journaling, every lesson, and each spicy meatball prepared has been done for one purpose—to bring you closer to understanding how vast God's love is for you and to equip you to better share that love with those in your life.

The greatest gift you can give someone is the gift of God's love. When you do, you position them to hear from God Himself, through you!

The world will tell you some are undeserving of love. Jesus tells you to love them anyway. The world will tell you that your sexual impulses are love. Jesus' definition of love is not impulsive; it's a choice. The world will tell you that love is about you. Jesus says love is about others.

In *Radical Love* we dug deep into God's word to reveal what He says about your purpose on this earth. To sum it up, your purpose is twofold:

1.) Be reconciled to God through Jesus Christ.
2.) Once saved, go and help save others.

It is that simple. 2 Corinthians 5:20 reads: *"Therefore, we are ambassadors for Christ, as though God were making an appeal through us; we beg you on behalf of Christ: be reconciled to God."*

It can't get any clearer than that, can it? Anytime you hold on to junk in your heart that clogs your ears from hearing from the Holy Spirit, you are not in a position to fulfill your ministry of reconciliation. You won't have the direct line to the guidance from the Spirit to notice the lonely woman who needs encouragement. You will be too busy plotting your revenge to see that your own son or daughter has had a bad day and needs to talk. You will be trying to make yourself happy instead of seeing who around you needs Jesus.

When God's love is skewed in your own life, the salvation of others is at stake! That's a tough meatball to swallow. But it is true.

Jesus was criticized, mocked, beaten, spat upon, and ultimately killed, but know this—He was not a victim. And when you choose to do it His way, neither are you. He chose to love others. He chose to speak the truth about who God was, no matter what the cost. He chose to love the unlovables. Will you?

God does not promise that when you show love to others, that you will be loved by them in return. Will you put your big kid shoes on anyway and step out in faith? God's promise is that when you do it His way, you will be loved by Him. Is that enough?

As you work through this final session, we pray you have already been forever changed by Christ's radical love. Over these past 8 sessions, maybe you've found youself acting in ways you know you could have never acted but by the strength of God in you. We cheer you on! There is one goal: The upward, heavenly call of God through Christ Jesus. For you and for as many as you can help get there through your ministry of reconciliation.

THE SPICY MEATBALL...
There will be times when what is in the best interest of someone else—the thing that shows God's love—will not be the thing you want to do.

1. How does the above statement resonate with you?

SCRIPTURE STUDY

At one point during Paul's second missionary journey he traveled through Philippi. While there, God used him and Silas to heal a slave girl, who was a fortune-teller for her masters. The masters were mad because her healing took away a source of their income. They had Paul and Silas beaten and imprisoned. That is the setting for this passage:

Acts 16:23-30:
23 *When they had struck them with many blows, they threw them into prison, commanding the jailer to guard them securely;* 24 *and he, having received such a command, threw them into the inner prison and fastened their feet in the stocks.*

25 *But about midnight Paul and Silas were praying and singing hymns of praise to God, and the prisoners were listening to them;* 26 *and suddenly there came a great earthquake, so that the foundations of the prison house were shaken; and immediately all the doors were opened and everyone's chains were unfastened.* 27 *When the jailer awoke and saw the prison doors opened, he drew his sword and was about to kill himself, supposing that the prisoners had escaped.* 28 *But Paul cried out with a loud voice, saying, "Do not harm yourself, for we are all here!"* 29 *And he called for lights and rushed in, and trembling with fear he fell down before Paul and Silas,* 30 *and after he brought them out, he said, "Sirs, what must I do to be saved?"*

2. What were Paul and Silas doing right before the earthquake happened?

3. Who else was present?

4. What happened to the prison after the earthquake?

5. What was the jailer's initial reaction and why? Were his initial assumptions correct?

6. What was his response when he saw that everyone was still there?

In Acts 12, we read that Peter was in prison. He was to be brought before Herod. Without warning, Peter's chains fell off. An angel of the LORD told him to escape. There is no doubt that Paul and Silas would have heard about this miraculous escape. When their chains fell off, none of us would have blinked an eye if they had taken that opportunity to escape too, right? But they stayed put.

7. How do you think Paul and Silas knew that staying in that prison, even though their chains fell off, was the right decision?

8. Do you think that the answer you gave for question 2
had anything to do with Paul and Silas knowing how to
respond in the earthquake? Explain.

1 Corinthians 2:14-16:
14 *But a natural man does not accept the things of the Spirit
of God, for they are foolishness to him; and he cannot
understand them, because they are spiritually appraised.*
15 *But he who is spiritual appraises all things, yet he himself
is appraised by no one.* 16 *For who has known the mind of
the LORD, that he will instruct him? But we have the mind of
Christ.*

9. Whose mind do you think Paul and Silas were linked
with at the moment they were in the prison?

Paul and Silas were led by the Holy Spirit. Acts 16:25 told
us they were praying and singing hymns in the presence of
the other prisoners. They abided in Christ, even in their
imprisonment! As such, God showed them what to do.

They did what was in the best interest, not for themselves, but for the jailer! He got saved! The human mind would have told them to run and get away when given the opportunity.

LIFE APPLICATION

10. Do you feel imprisoned by a person or a circumstance? What is confining you?

11. Do you believe that if you stay connected to Christ, if you abide in Him through all of the ways we've studied in this book, that you will be able to know Christ's love response that will free you from your imprisonment? Explain.

(Space for question 11)

12. Do you feel better equipped to love others the way
Jesus loves you than you did before you began this study?
How?

JOURNAL
Write a letter of commitment to God. Include confession, repentance, declarations of forgiveness, release of envy, control, or mistrust, whatever God has spoken to you strongly about over the past sessions, give it back to Him. End with statements of worship and acceptance of His promises.

CLOSING THOUGHTS

We said this in *Radical Love*, so you may have heard it before, but it bears repeating. If you are a child of God, then the **only** power Satan has over you is to tempt you with deception. He may orchestrate storms in your life. He may whisper lies into your ear. He may lure those you love to put their focus elsewhere. And friend, it might be awful! BUT, Satan cannot force you to sin. He can only tempt you to do so. The power in you is greater than the power of Satan. Do you believe that? Do you believe Jesus has more power than Satan? Guess what? That same power resides in you. It came along with the Holy Spirit on the day you accepted Jesus and repented of your sins. You can be victorious no matter what. NO MATTER WHAT!

Say this out loud: **"I can be victorious no matter what."**

When you pick up the cross of Christ every day, you choose to pick up His love, His power, and His heart for others. You choose to say, "OK Jesus, it might be hard, it might not make sense to my human mind, but I'm doing things Your way today."

It's a daily choice. The world will tell you to continually place yourself at the center. The world will tempt you to be envious, mistrusting, controlling, fearful, and angry. The world will show you why you should blame others for your challenges.

Here's something you can cling to: You've been told the end of the story for each problem you face. God wins. He prevails. He succeeds. Your job is to remain in Christ's love by abiding in Him. Do it His way and you can't go wrong.

Nothing crushes Satan's plans harder than when God's people show God's love to the ones Satan is trying hard to destroy. It sends Satan back to hell when we are a part of someone else's salvation story. Your purpose is not simply to avoid the evil in this world, but whenever possible to overcome it with His love.

God loves you.

Leader's Notes

You may have heard it said that if you make yourself available, God will give you the ability. A willing servant is a blessing to many. With your willingness to serve as a group leader, you simultaneously must commit to preparing before each group time. The leader sets the example for the group. When a leader shows up and declares, "I didn't even look at this week's lesson," you are saying to the group, "This really isn't all that important to me." Soon, you'll notice others in the group stop doing their lessons too. And the group falls apart.

You don't have to be a biblical scholar to lead a small group. You do need a love for Jesus and the willingness to do your part. We pray these next pages will help you as you prepare for each small group gathering. Collectively, we have led hundreds of men and women through small group experiences. We have seen groups thrive and groups fail. In this section we'll provide you with some general tips, followed by session-specific notes.

GENERAL NOTES

- Be prepared. As mentioned above, the rest of the group may or may not complete the session work, but you need to set the example by being ready.
- Identify a back-up. Is there someone in the group who would be available to step up in case you have a sick child, emergency, or other problem arise at the last minute? Identify that person before the group

even begins.

- If your small group includes snacks or food, give everyone a 2 minute warning to freshen coffee, get their plate, and find their seat before you begin.
- As the leader, be the one to open study time with prayer. If you are the one praying, then you have the floor, so to speak, and you can move right into the lesson following your prayer.
- You are the guide, but the journey is about the group. As such, each lesson includes a mix of discussion questions with questions that can be learned right from Scripture. Discussion about real-life gives opportunity for discipleship.
- Ask a question, then be patient for an answer. If your group is hesitant to answer a question, politely give some space for the Spirit to prompt someone to speak up. Don't rush in and answer your own question.
- Do not force someone to talk if they truly do not want to. It may have been a huge step of faith for someone to even show up. Never bully someone into answering a question.
- Bring it back to the Bible. Everyone has an opinion, and we don't want to confuse our opinions with what God says. Don't be afraid to say, "That's an interesting viewpoint. Why don't we see what God says on the matter?"
- Don't be afraid to "shelf" a question and tell someone that you don't know the answer at the moment, but you will see what the Bible says and will reply at the next session. Remember, you aren't expected to know everything. Don't answer something if you aren't sure. Find an expert to help. (Pastor, trusted biblical source, commentaries)
- Decide ahead of time the time frame and structure. Don't work on the fly. Your group will appreciate

when you adhere to a schedule.
- Leave time for fellowship.
- End the official study time with prayer.
- Send an encouraging e-mail or text midway between study gatherings, so members know you are thinking about them. It may also prompt them to work on their lessons.
- Ask God to show you what you need to know about those in your group. He has a purpose for you and for each one there. Ask Him to reveal it to you and be willing to engage with those He brings to you.

SAMPLE GROUP OUTLINE

This suggestion for your group time is based on our experience and this specific study.

1.) Prayer.
2.) Highlight passages from the **Lesson Introduction** that stood out to you. Read them out loud.
3.) Read the **Spicy Meatball** statement. Ask the group to share how the statement made them feel.
4.) Use the Session information beginning on the next page to support your discussion on the **Scripture Study** questions. For each session, we also include additional scripture passages you may want to have group members look up, read out loud, and discuss.
5.) Choose one or more of the **Life Application** questions from that session's study. Read aloud and ask if anyone wants to share. Be ready to give your own answer or an example to kickstart discussion if necessary.
6.) Ask one or more of the following questions:

- What has God shown you this week that is new from His word?

- What stood out the most to you in this session's lesson?
- Did this session's study bring to mind any specific situations or experiences you've had that maybe you haven't thought about in a long time?
- Did your thinking about the Spicy Meatball change after going through the lesson? If so, how?
- Is there anything you've committed to God to do differently as a result of this lesson? If so, what?
- Was there anything in the content that was unclear or that formed new questions in your mind? What are they?

7.) Close with prayer.

SCRIPTURE STUDY COMMENTS:

SESSION 1: Examine Your Expectations

The idea of laying aside our expectations is difficult. There are many things we "expect" in life. We expect our boss to give us a paycheck when it's due. We expect our kids to behave in school. We expect our days to go, for the most part, as planned. False expectations lead to trouble. Our expectations of what God will or won't do can lead to a barrier between us and God.

Our expectations get us in trouble because God's way of doing things is vastly different from how we would do them. Ask the group to share when their misplaced expectations had led to disappointment and ask the group to commit to laying down expectations for the weeks of this study and to be open to anything God may want to show them.

Read and discuss how these verses relate to Expectations:
Philippians 1:20
James 4:13-15
Proverbs 10:28
Proverbs 16:2
1 Samuel 16:7

SESSION 2: Examine Your Obedience

In the introduction to this lesson, we suggested the importance of conducting a regular heart-check to look for areas where your soul might be showing signs of sickness. Areas of rebellion are a sure sign that you need to pay attention to your heart.

If you have time, read Deuteronomy 11. Discuss how the Israelites' obedience was important to their success in the Promised Land. What parallels can the group make to Christians today?

Read and discuss how these verses relate to Obedience:
Exodus 19:5
Luke 11:28
James 1:25
Romans 2:6-8
James 4:17

SESSION 3: Examine Your Salvation

The passage from Matthew 7:21-23 is quite difficult for some to bear. Our instinct is to think of a loved one who may have fallen away from the church. The group may get into a discussion about who is saved and who is not.

"I know my son is saved because he prayed the sinner's prayer and was baptized!" You will hear this comment (or a

version of it.)

None of us like to think of a loved one as unsaved. We'd be monsters if we didn't care about the salvation of our kids, relatives, family, or friends. Have someone from the group read Matthew 13:24-30 and the Matthew 13:36-43. It is the parable of the wheat and tares. Emphasize that God alone knows the heart condition of each person. He knows if someone offers lip service or if there is true heart change. Our job is not to point fingers. Our job is to make sure our individual hearts are right and then to go and make disciples with Jesus' story. If someone we love is currently not walking with Jesus, we are to continue to shine Christ's light to that person. Instead of getting into a discussion about "who is saved" a good idea would be to talk about how we can show Christ's love to those in our lives who are not walking with the Lord; yes, even those who have said a "sinner's prayer."

Read and discuss how these verses relate to Salvation:
Psalm 27:1
Romans 10:9-10
Hebrews 7:25
Psalm 37:39
Daniel 6:16

SESSION 4: Examine Your Motives

In Philippians 2, Paul instructs that we are to do nothing with selfishness as a motive. Nada. Zip. Ask the group to talk about times when they may feel being selfish is OK. How do their answers line up with Scripture?

This lesson is difficult to put into practice because we constantly want to think about how WE are affected in all situations.

The key point to make with the group is that if they remain connected to Christ, the Spirit will warn them when their motives are not Christ-centered. When we get the warning, we'll have a choice to make. That moment of decision is where we show our faith in God for an outcome. Ask if they can think of a time when they knew they had a choice between two things and they picked the one that made things "easiest" for them, even though deep down they knew they should do the other one.

Read and discuss how these verses relate to Motives:
Proverbs 21:2
Galatians 1:10
Matthew 6:1
1 Samuel 16:7
Colossians 3:17

SESSION 5: Examine Your Trust

When we learn to recognize that control, fear, anxiety, worry, and panic are warning signs that we lack trust in God, our entire lives will change.

The Israelites' lack of faith give a wonderfully clear example of this. The story of Peter walking on water (Matthew 14:22-33) is another example of someone who began to do something miraculous, but let his fear of the storm overwhelm him. The good news is that Peter reached for Jesus and Jesus righted him on the water.

Like Peter, we need to take concrete steps to connect with Jesus when fear, control, worry, anxiety, or panic pop up in our emotional state. Talk with the group about what "connecting with Jesus" means to them. Make it very practical.

Read and discuss how these verses relate to Trust:
Nahum 1:7
Psalm 9:10
Daniel 6:23
Romans 15:13
Revelation 21:5

SESSION 6: Examine Your Temper

We all know someone who has a worse temper than we do!
The temptation for the group might be to tell "people who
have shown a bad temper" stories. As leader, try and keep
the focus on controlling our OWN tempers. Looking at the
situations when WE lose our temper, and what can we do
about it.

In Proverbs 15:1 we read: *A gentle answer turns away
wrath, but a harsh word stirs up anger.*

Ask for examples of a time when someone may have
wanted to respond with bitterness, but they gave a calm,
gentle word and it diffused the situation.

In Genesis 37, we read of Joseph's brothers selling him into
slavery. It was their anger that drove them to such action.
Yet years later, in Genesis 42-45, Joseph is faced with his
brothers again and comes to the emotional place where he
forgives them. It wasn't an easy journey for Joseph. Discuss
how Joseph controlled his temper when faced with his
brothers and the truth that Joseph clung to that enabled
him to forgive. (Find it in Genesis 45:3-8)

Read and discuss how these verses relate to Temper:
Timothy 2:24
Proverbs 14:17
Galatians 15:19-20

Luke 4:28-29
Proverbs 22:24-25

SESSION 7: Examine Your Mercy

How does the statement Jesus makes in Matthew 18:35 sit
with the members of the group? Is it a tough truth? What
Jesus is saying is that we do not understand how great
salvation is if we are unable to forgive others. We won't
always get it right; but in increasing measures, we should
find ourselves growing in mercy, compassion, and love for
those around us. If we are not, then we really don't
understand how big of a sacrifice Jesus made on our own
behalf.

The little book of Jude has more to say about why mercy is
necessary. It is evangelical in that Jude gives a forewarning
of what is to come for the unbeliever. So, we must show
mercy in order to help the unbeliever find salvation. Read
Jude 1:17-23 to the group and discuss.

Read and discuss how these verses relate to Mercy:
Hebrews 4:16
1 Peter 1:3
2 Samuel 24:14
Luke 6:36
Matthew 5:7

SESSION 8: Examine Your Love

Use this final group time to celebrate the new truths that
each one has learned as related to their personal
understanding of Jesus' love. If someone has done even one
of the lessons in the study, then we are confident that God
has had a word to say to them.

Use this time as a time of review, to address any points you may have not gotten to because of time constraints, and celebrate any barriers that have been broken. In the first session, we asked if the group would be willing to set aside their expectations and preconceived ideals. Did they do this? What did God show them?

End with prayer. We would love to hear your success stories and comments.

Connect with us

Donna Lowe

www.DonnaLowe.com

Kimberly Soesbee

www.KimberlySoesbee.com